THE EPHE

GW01091269

THE
EPHEMERAL
ISLE

AUDREY SCALES

PORTMOON PRESS

First published 1983
Reprinted 1983

Published by Portmoon Press,
PO Box 9, Limavady,
Co. Londonderry, BT49 9AJ

British Library Cataloguing in Publication Data

Scales, Audrey

    The ephemeral isle.
    I.Title
    823'.914[F]   PR6069.C/

    ISBN 0-9508551-0-3

Printed in Northern Ireland
by The Universities Press (Belfast) Ltd.

For my family
and friends

"There's night and day, brother, both sweet things; sun, moon, and stars, brother, all sweet things; there's likewise a wind on the heath. Life is very sweet, brother; who would wish to die?"

George Borrow, *Lavengro*

CONTENTS

UNDER THE SKY

UNDER THE SKIN

ACKNOWLEDGEMENTS

I should like to thank: Martyn Anglesea of the Department of Art, Ulster Museum, Professor Anne Crookshank of Trinity College, Dublin, and the Knight of Glin for their help in providing the cover illustrations; Barbara Lane and Cilla Stevenson for their encouragement; and Judith Vinycomb for her invaluable editorial assistance.

Audrey Scales
Limavady, 1983

To the Reader

A spontaneous offering, this small token,
Maybe you would prefer it spoken,
Or yet enjoy the written word –
Of pleasure, or the plain absurd,
Of thoughts that pulse below the skin,
Of beneficial wandering,
Of people, places, under the sky –
To reward your interest I will try
To suit my song to your bent
And fulfil my intent
Should a Reader's fleeting smile
Shine upon *The Ephemeral Isle*.

THE EPHEMERAL ISLE

Isle of Doagh

They are making hay
At Trawbreaga bay;
An old lady is making butter,
Ambrosial butter,
A round pat, embossed with a flower.
Someone is cutting willows
To make turf baskets.
Cottage thatches are immaculate
Beneath Atlantic hairnets;
So will be the haystacks
When the hay is dry.

White thyme and purple
Spreads over lane edges,
A star of bog asphodel
Gleams orange among rushes.
Meadowsweet at our feet,
Fuchsia bobs in the air,
Pale mountains of Urris
Are another day's promise.

Straight as arrows mallard fly
The length of the land-locked bay.
On a bank of yellow-lichened rock
I open my paintbox;
The sky is in the sand
Where cockles hide.
A curlew curlews
As you gather mussels.

Inishowen Revisited

Around the yellow house at Carrignoc
Nobody needs to cut the grass
Which humps and hollows smoothly to the rocks
Beside a sandy cove.

The dormer window looks across the water
To the craggy curve of benevolent Benevenagh.
Does it remember
A pre-war summer –
Twin brothers with bicycles,
Excited escapees from school and town,
Scramble off a train at the Halt,
Pedal fast to the tower on the point
And take a ferry boat across the narrows.

Skinny brown bodies in swimming trunks
Run helter skelter to the water,
Swim, duck-dive,
Wave to the passengers
Of a transatlantic liner throbbing by.

They cycle express to the village,
Dawdle back licking cornets of ice-cream.
Sitting on the rocks one day
Is a young boy's dream –
Friendly smiles and careless hair:
Two sisters;
One is painting a picture
With a feather.

The New Donegal

Where has the honeysuckle gone?
And the wild roses
In fuchsia hedges
Among fern and campion?

Who brought this barren autobahn
To our lush island,
This Mid-West corral fencing
To windswept Ireland?

Hard shoulders – yes,
Hard heads too,
And hard noses.
They make us
Paupers.

The Walled Garden

Mountain cliffs a mile away look down
On a square of mellow brick walls.
A fountain plays in a small round pool
In a pattern of roses and miniature hedges;
Ornamental iron chairs
Surround a sun-dial, its slate face cracked.
Mimosa waves through the roof
Of a collapsing Gothic greenhouse.

Green grapes turn purple slowly
In wet autumn days;
Tiger lilies shake their turbanned heads.
Furry caterpillars feed
On broccoli long gone to seed.

A wooden door in the high brick wall
Bursts open and a dog bounds in;
His owners are away.
A wild cat and her kittens vanish,
A rabbit heads for his hole.

Among soft fronds of asparagus
Strange pink poppies bloom;
Sea mists have grown grey lichen
On tall apple trees.
A secret underworld feasts on windfalls:
The owners are away.

Hang Glider

The tufts of grass seem real
But my feet don't stumble –
The wind is carrying me
Above the ground.
My toes touch a boulder
And brush the back of a sheep:
Its Roman nose and glassy eyes
Are clear. It runs away
Its fat tail shaking.
What monster magpie am I
Or giant cattle egret
About to settle
And peck the parasites out of its wool?

The harness tightens, my wings fill and lift –
A moment treading air, a helpless object,
Now horizontal, comfortably air-cushioned,
I float above a spacious landscape.
Tiny figures wave far below.

Cold wet mist flows over my face –
The edge of a cloud.
The cliffs glide past.
Two fulmars on a ledge, like doves,
Lift off in effortless flight, encircling me
With curious beaks and eyes.
Something cries: a buzzard maybe,
Large and brown
It wails again, calling its mate –
Has this strange new bird come to prey?

Stone Circles at Beaghmore, Co. Tyrone

Take this wide scroll of moorland,
These outlines of bog grass and brown heather;
Take a brush and daub and stipple
Thick as paint will stick on bare canvas –
Make trees, clustered and dense,
A mixed and mottled forest over all.
Leave a clearing here, where we stand.

As you might draw a breath through your teeth
So the wind hisses
Among these circles of stone.
They wait, like people watching, taking part
In some ritual never to be known.
One circle is crowded with stones on end:
A mass memorial of battle –
Chevaux de frise to guard a chieftain's tomb –
A tribal census, a tally of years –
A plan of the planets and stars?

The mind goes into a falling spin
Through aeons and aeons;
The world tilts, turns over,
Populations and cities fall away –
We are left with land and water, sun and moon.
The horizon is there for the taking.

Does the sun shine? Occasionally
A white hole in the mist can be perceived.
Diffuse grey light becomes a lurid glow;
The land comes to life
With the benefit of shadow.
In days of good omen, days of the sun god,
Horned beasts lumber to the river,
Wild-haired people gather for barter,
Wizen-faced offspring cling.
How many handfuls of grain for a flint?
Is a clay pot worth a fur hide?

The stony silence tells us nothing;
Yet these surviving witnesses
Render us as fleeting as bog cotton
Blossoming in June and in August gone.

Iris

Regal purple rises from a clutch of swords:
A chalice, a triumvirate of minuscule beards;
Velvet robe embroidered with a swarm of bees,
Emblem of France, the fleur-de-lis.

Yellow flags are out in meadow marshes
By the alder-dark river, lighting up the rushes;
The Light of the North – once Ireland's reputation,
Brief as a dragonfly's gossamer scintillation.

A House in Ireland

Beyond the terrace an arboretum burgeons
Concealing paths that peter out in swamp;
In fountainless alcove bittersweet hangs,
A red rose runs riot around an urn.

The shuttered house sees nothing: it waits
Like the old portraits, holds its memories
Of fires in winter bedrooms, laundry maids,
Upswept hair, white hands and tapestries.

No bell clangs above the carriage yard,
No hooves paw the floor to get out;
Termites riddle a mouldering side-saddle
Among straw and lath of subsiding hayloft.

Doors grate open into empty byres;
Bullocks graze in safe stockade –
The walled garden: a toppled sun-dial lies,
Framed by espaliers, gnarled and dead.

Ivy has made hedges of stone walls,
Tongued with fern, haunt of shrews
And tree-creepers. As night falls,
A hunting owl glides through the copse.

The Syndicate

Brilliant birds of autumn colour,
Burnished bronze and red-gold fire,
Cackle on the balustrade –
Lords of the demesne.

Pheasant hens of speckled dun
Forage on the sodden lawn;
Incredulous cats watch wistfully
The inconveniently feathered food.

Mud-green men in down-turned headgear
Pour hot coffee in the morning mist;
Spaniels wag their tailored tails,
Beaters are briefed on how to yell.

Raucous sounds of a warring street-gang
Put to flight the tame corn-fed birds;
Great trees shiver as the shots blast out –
Limp little bodies hang on the cart.

They don't stalk their prey, the cult-clad sportsmen,
Keen confederates in gruesome pursuit
A bevy of farmer's wives gone berserk
Gunning down Rhode Island Reds.

A Faint Smell of Spring

In the garden winter will soon be over:
A hint of honey blows from snowdrops
Spread like damask for a fête champêtre.
Triumphantly a pheasant celebrates freedom.

The stout king beech still wears his filigree crown,
His caryatid queen supports one classic arm;
In his wide circle of moss and crinkled lichen
Apricot chanterelle sprouted last autumn.

Glistening buds of sinuous chestnut
Will make fans and fishtails in long-grassed summer;
Come out, Celandine – only a few weeks left
Before shade will steal your gold treasure.

In a swampy clearing by the brown foaming river
Peaked yellow hoods push up through the mud:
The musky mantle of skunk lily —
A ghost of gaslight pervades the dank air.

Moondrops of mahonia shine beneath dark yews,
Fragrant foretaste of a warmer season;
In the happy aroma of incense cedar
A voluptuous thrush proclaims his territory.

Lovely Hobby

Watery eyes the March wind gave,
Tingling hands and frozen nose;
I dug the ground and trenches made
To bury manure in tidy rows.

In April's flashing sun and showers
I calculated crop rotation,
Drew neat drills and for some hours
Sowed seed in happy expectation.

One day in June was tropically hot,
I crawled about through lush new green
Dead-nettle, fumitory, forget-me-not –
My vegetables could not be seen.

"How's it going?" she called from her chestnut mare,
I straightened up, groaned "It'll take all day" –
Black hunting cap on curly fair hair
"Lovely hobby" she said, as she rode away.

13

Spring Candlemas

The lawn is a lake of blue speedwell,
Rippling and whitening with sea-like swell,
Tiny flowers tinted from miniature inkwell;
A host of eyes mesmerise, cast a spell.

Chestnut leaf shuttlecocks sway, and say:
"Wait till you see my display –
The bladed monster will cut you away –
But I am the Christmas tree of May."

Azalea

Foam of flame
And tangerine,
Fiery trumpets:
Rose, vermilion;
Ripened peach
In pearly vapour –
Smell sweet honey-gold
Azalea.

May Queen

Spin me a dress of light green silk,
Let me wade in a bluebell lake,
Or walk on petal-drifted grass
And watch the new world wake.

Spread me a cloth of Queen Anne's Lace
Where ferns uncurl through the hours;
Pour mead wine into bright buttercups
By the glow of sycamore flowers.

Paint me a daisy: golden face,
White ruff, rose-tinted edges;
Give me sun's image, dandelion,
And cream of hawthorn hedges.

Hatch me a nest of open beaks,
Small feathers about to fly;
Carry me off on a passing cloud,
The only one in the sky.

Summer

On a halcyon day
Soft air strokes the plume-topped hay,
Bees drink deep in tufted clover,
Pigeons murmur "summer, summer";
From a haze of shimmering green
Grasshoppers sickle unseen.
Juicy grass is damp on skin –
Cool pillow for restless fiend within;
Busy-ness is lost to the sky
In the soul of a black zig-zagging fly.

"Wind of Clynder"

A seagull on the waves, my ship,
Her bow wave translucent green,
With goose-winged jib she flies through foam,
To windward she slices clean.

In the cabin are cushions and polished wood,
Compass, echo-sounder and radio,
Galley and bunks, and a bulkhead beyond,
Charts and books and my lady-o.

Between Scotland west and Ireland north
Is a choppy stretch of ocean,
Enough to call for a fair measure
Of skill in sail and navigation.

In the greying light she glides out,
Coastal buoys blink their warning;
She careens high and low through Atlantic swell
Until the line of landfall at morning.

The dark lonely cockpit becomes a verandah:
Oilskins off and stretch in the sun;
As she rides quietly at anchor
Thanksgiving breakfast has begun.

Tales of the Equinox

Calves cavort across the field –
Tails up like carnival torches;
A young horse high-steps it about –
Tail up like a flag,
Head-tossing, snorting,
The wind in his ears.

Cats caper after leaves –
Tails up like plumes,
Shooting up the spreading yew tree
With supersonic ease.

Conkers canon down,
Bunting flaps on a tangled wash-line,
Flowers blow through the air;
Life whirls about
In a crazy pageant –
Autumn is here.

Autumn Day

Glancing morning sun of late October
Vivifies small pittings in a sandstone wall;
The swallows have left, chestnut leaves lie deeper,
A parading pheasant shouts his clatter-call.

The year is dressed in evening array:
Diaphanous mist, diamantine cobweb,
Cloth of gold, attar of amber and honey,
Polished berry beads of jet and garnet.

Moss makes velvet north trunks and fallen branches,
Iridescent green in lessening leaf shade;
Puffballs transmogrify to mammoth sponges,
Spores disperse as dust to dust is laid.

November Zombie

Late in the year, in Hibernia,
A semi-hibernating creature,
Neither awake nor asleep,
Weighed down by cloud,
Crosses waterlogged land
Among grey perspectives of bare trees,
Past silent houses
To street lamps glittering in drizzle.
A seagull mews and wheels
In search of crust or carrion.

Routine momentum briefly halts;
The creature, trailing a wraith of mist,
Slithers from its mechanical shell
To a brass slit in the wall –
A phantom hand takes the proffered letter.
Somewhere nearby
A human being cooks bacon.
Resuming its cocoon
The creature joins a queue of glow-worms
Receding to vanishing point.

How harsh the fluorescent brilliance,
All too clear the delimitations of the building;
The creature, loth to leave its element,
The no-world of half-light beyond the windows,
Envies its brothers in spirit –
Fluffed-out clusters of black feathers–
Rooks roosting on the factory fence.

A Gale in the Bamboo

Sound of a thousand waterfalls –
All around
Sway the great swathes
Of bamboo.

Green wands, green feathers,
Wild weather endeavours
To pluck the long plumes
Of bamboo.

People who pass
Through the forest of grass
Are hustled and tousled,
Bamboozled and lost.

Wandering mandarin,
Pigtail and parasol,
Paintbrush and silk scroll,
Blown away all.

Strong boat, dry house,
Plump duck and big fish;
Feed us and shelter us,
Kind bamboo.

Under verandah
A family of panda;
Bring us luck, bring us joy,
Honoured bamboo.

Catch the wind, snatch the wind,
Myriad leaves match the wind;
Seek not the secrets
Behind bamboo.

Private View

Blurred fur looms large,
Glossy hair tosses on silky dresses,
Glasses of wine float by.

Happy squawks accompany mutual recognition:
Powdered faces embrace with ritual affection.
Pin-headed patron in pin-striped suit
Weaves towards spike-heeled sandals
Eyeing with interest her elegant ankles.
Norfolk-jacketed leather-faced dealer
Stands silent beside spotty protégé.

Gold lamé talks to shiny white oilskin,
Suède skirt swings under oriental sheepskin,
Wooden beads rattle on hessian caftan,
Blue-rinsed coiffure crowns impeccable tailoring.

Coloured laces criss-cross the bare feet
Of blue-eyed popsies
Skipping about
In pastel muslin nightdresses.
Female intelligentsia peer
Through uniform fringes on forehead:
"Art for me is a terribly visual thing,"
One said.

Someone heard a businessman declare
"I shall buy a picture in England –
They're half the price over there."
An urbane host greets late arrivals
With a slightly anxious air
(Dinner will be very late tonight, I fear).

The bemused artist shakes hands politely,
Answers questions patiently,
Discusses technique professionally.
Maybe, also,
He is thinking, wistfully,
That with all this animated distraction
His paintings seem only a fraction
Of the general show.

Under the Chestnut Tree

Handsome red tractor is here –
Happy market day –
Blue dungarees are in the air,
Gumboots are coming this way.

Who would have thought
She'd have had her heart turned over
By the sound of cattle bought,
Ruddy face, ragged pullover.

She covets the clinching handshakes,
A shy young farmer's daughter;
If she were a lamb, she speculates,
He could easily have bought her.

The New University of Ulster

South from this hill
A town is banked about a river
With bridge, and quay, and sandstone clock tower;
A grass fort guards the willowed upper reaches.

North, sand hills in a haze of spume
Deflect for a mile or two
The river's ocean escape.

On this auspicious hill
Unrelated structures stagger across the skyline,
Desolate, windswept, dropped from somewhere
By God knows whom.
Glass passages snake over bare terrain
Lacking only unconscious patients on stretchers.

Within, a catacomb engulfs us,
Minus daylight, minus air,
The "gods" of some seedy opera house?
A lecture theatre.

Coke and comics hide the coffee tables,
Rows of easy chairs confront the telly
Beneath a floor suspended in mid-air
Reached by a Piranesian staircase
Past penny-in-the-slot football.
An airport terminal, hotel foyer?
The college forum.
Species adapt to their habitat.

Where are the great builders?
Must the discerning eyes of our nation
Remain forever fossilized in bog?

Megalithic supermen,
Spirits of Dundrum,
Visionaries of gentle Mellifont:
Don't look, don't look at this,
This cardboard mock-up, this misconception,
This lost opportunity.

I dreamt of a citadel, worthy of Saladin,
Growing on this hill,
A continuous bulwark against the climate
Of this northerly outpost;
Its rooms full of light, looking out upon the world,
Looking in upon its quiet interior.
Through an arched gateway I glimpsed
Colonnades and paved courtyards,
One beyond another.
I heard a bird sing and a campanile chime
And a murmur of distant voices.

Marsh Gas

Town of friendly lakeland people,
Enniskillen floats;
Fan-lights, Redoubt and moats,
Castle, cannon and steeple.

Encircling hills gnash rows of teeth,
Housing estated
Desecrated.
For a lost skyline, in the lake throw a wreath.

Why have we come, what do we need?
Mr. Knott gives good measure
On wide wooden counter
Of living, breathing tweed.

"That piece I took – may I have a bit more?"
"Ah, that's a favourite –
I was preserving it –"
It is fetched from a secret store.

City-suited kind owner of the Royal bar,
Hot toddy and sandwiches
Between televised horse races –
"It's a raw day. Have you come far?"

Three generations of Armstrong
Are in attendance
Selling clothes of elegance
In their tawny-carpeted salon.

We choose an oriental silk tie;
"Your Uncle Hal?
I knew him well.
Used to play tennis together, he and I."

There's Gloucester House beyond the trees,
The memorial gates of Portora.
Picture a small brother:
Blazer, cap and muddy knees.

The colonnades of Castlecoole
Stand on the wet field,
Incongruously revealed:
A white elephant, but beautiful.

Great Aunt Fanny

The creek at Killybegs glistened
In the early morning sun,
On the quay with his daughter Fanny
Stood Captain Robert Hamilton.
Tall masts towered above them,
Sheets and halyards gently tapping,
Around the great oak hull
A new breeze brought small waves lapping.

In homespun cape and long full skirt
Fanny sniffed the salty air;
As the Captain watched the hold fill up,
His stomach felt emptier.
They had said goodbye to Martha,
Who couldn't bear to come
And wave away her daughter
To sail so far from home.

She was sweet eighteen with soft brown eyes
And brown hair curling down,
A spirited girl and full of fun
But never been beyond the town.
And now they were bound for Chile,
For Valparaiso port;
A pity not to take the chance,
Both she and parents thought.

The voyage would be long and arduous,
Wet and cold and rough,
But these people of Donegal
Were accustomed to being tough.
Home-cured ham and galley-baked bread
Would help the good crew sing
For the nine thousand miles they were to sail
To where autumn was spring.

Last time when Captain Hamilton
Sailed around the world,
With cargoes to exchange
At Valparaiso he called.
A young man came aboard
And invited him home to dine –
It was Mr. Henry Jones, manager
Of a local copper mine.

As they rode to the house the sunset glowed
On the snow-capped Cordillera,
Among vines and eucalyptus
Henry lived in lonely splendour.
The Captain talked of Ireland,
Of his wife and daughters at home,
And Henry of his hopes and plans
In the country he'd made his own.

The two had much in common,
And before they retired to rest,
With hesitation Henry made
A curious request:
Next time the Captain came
Would he bring a daughter for company,
With the tentative, almost unspoken, purpose
Of possible matrimony.

Fanny was her father's daughter:
The wide world held great attraction;
The thrilling choice was offered –
Not a difficult decision.
So here they were in Killybegs
This fine October day,
The taut ropes creaked, the canvas cracked,
The good ship sailed away.

Wild Wine

Sniff the bouquet of a southerly clime:
Mavrodaphne, Muscatel,
Topaz glint of elderflower wine
Cooled in some Arcadian well.

Faery-fermented pellet-grape,
Harvest of uncut hedgerow,
Elixir of unreal escape –
The purple liquid let flow.

How come this blossom froths and fruits
In our inhospitable north?
A lost memory of idyllic pursuits
Impels us to set forth.

Song: The Brown River Roe

On the rocky banks of the brown river Roe
I met my love, long long ago.
Wading in the water he was nearly swept away;
I sat and watched all the livelong day.

The sunlight shone through the fresh green leaves,
Deep pools were dark beneath the trees;
A silver sea-trout rose to take a fly –
But not the one that would have made it die.

Then we walked and talked and the river ran by,
And I was the fish and he was the fly;
How handsomely he cast and how readily I rose –
Caught for a lifetime and so the river flows.

Song: Mountain Dew

Oh Benevenagh
How far to heaven-ah?
Take me with you
Drench me in mountain dew.

Sunny weather
For walking in the heather
Around Lough Foyle
Walk the sons of the soil.

Inishowen
Where are you going?
You seem to be
Heading out to sea.

Silver river
What will you give her?
A shoal of fish
And a secret wish.

Amber mountain lake
How long does it take
A trout to grow
Into a rainbow?

Birds in the rugged cliffs
Life is full of ifs
If only we could fly
We could live in the sky.

Dream of Samarkand
Miles of golden sand
Hide in the dunes
Lost for many moons.

Blue horizon
Who are you calling?
A far away land
Reaches out its hand.

Exchange of Views

For Zaza and Mahmud
on their visit to Northern Ireland

I

Limavahdia, they called it,
Evoking the eastern Mediterranean and beyond –
Mud houses in a wide dust road, shaded chai-khana,
Date plams, flame trees and jacaranda.
But no, we are here in Limavady,
The rain slides down horse-chestnut leaves,
It patters on sou'wester and umbrella,
It echoes in the Mussenden Temple.

Largantea – the name has unsuspected music,
A village among cotton fields in the Delta,
Not a public picnic area
Beside the old road to Coleraine.
A stream cascades between boulders and heather,
Narrowly bridged with rough timber.
Three score years and ten sit lightly
On Mahmud: he sketches busily, ecstatically –
"I will make this for my museum at Aswan!"
Aswan! Turbulent, sparkling cataract of the Nile,
Great sloping slabs of Elephantine Island
Spread with brightly coloured clothes
Drying in the scorching sun.

Largantea ... wet wood tables steam as misty sunlight
Pierces a hole in the clouds.
Hooded, in anoraks,
We warm our hands on mugs of tea.

The corniche in Alex was never busier nor happier
Than this windy small promontory into the Atlantic –
Portrush: the paddling pool and bumper boats are packed;
We join the ice-cream-licking rosy mob
And buy linen gifts for distant friends.

II

Shall we go to the Giant's Causeway
Even though it is August Bank Holiday?
The minibus overflows with a noisy happy horde,
But no black-veiled women, laden with baskets
Full of hens, vegetables and ducks.

It is a festival day, a Shemm en-Neseem:
The Day of Smelling the Wind –
Where are the scampering little girls
In shocking-pink spring dresses?
Where are the lads with shaven heads
Dazzling in striped new robes?

A deceptive calm sea swells quietly around;
Tee-shirts swarm over a honeycomb of rock.
What million minions hewed these hexagons?
At sixes and sevens they left them.
Faceted blocks of miniature pyramids
Level off to become tessellated ground,
Cooled, shrunk and solidified,
Disgorged from a fiery earth.

An olive-skinned French couple,
Pharaonic-featured, graceful,
Svelte in black and neutral,
Eloquently discuss geology.

Sunday-suited husband and high-heeled wife
Push a canopied pram to a convenient spot;
They sit, with Granny, gazing at the grassy cliff –
A huge amphitheatre curving to the headland.
Nobody tells us whose obelisk that is,
Nor offers us a camel to ride.

For two piastres we might sail in a felucca
To that settlement glinting where sea and sky meet –
But a motor fishing boat is all that we can see;
Strains of molten music drift across
From Scotland, twenty miles away.

Let's take the mid-cliff path to Dunseverick;
Too late for primroses, but there's an orchid.
Papyrus columns give us pause for thought:
Pale limestone has become black basalt.
Remember the Red Sea mountains – here's Roman porphyry –
But no, it's clay. Below, the wrecked Girona,
Watery tomb of weary sailors and lost treasure.

III

The Travellers bestow a wealth of new perceptions:
Illuminating memories, curious comparisons;
Invest us with gifts both tangible and wearable –
Silk-braided Berber waistcoat, bright galabeya-gown.
Sketches by Professor Architect are laid in portfolio,
A choice of purchases is packed by his lady.
The great silver bird roars, runs and soars
To retrace a few hours of the sun's recent course.
With a twist of the wrist the earth-ball shifts –
A different seam comes uppermost.

UNDER THE SKY

THE EPHEMERAL ISLE

by AUDREY SCALES

"An extensive range of poetry that should appeal to a cross-section of readers."
Belfast Telegraph

"Rich pages of writing ... not to be missed..."
Fermanagh Herald

"Direct and evocative; and readable. She has humour and wit."
Impartial Reporter

"A real pleasure to read."
Sunday Press

"...one can indeed call it poetry with a wide public appeal. In many poems the authoress shows herself to be romantic in an uncomplicated way ..."
PRISMA (Netherlands)

"Highly pleasurable ... the author displays elegance, charm and virtuosity."
Belfast Newsletter

"A delightful book"
Derry Journal

"She has a much wider experience than most contemporary Ulster poets and this familiarity with Baghdad and Isfahan is reflected in her poems."
British Book News

"A light touch ... the writer alternately delights and disconcerts."
County Down Spectator

"Full of interest ... this excellent breath of home and abroad."
Coleraine Chronicle

FIRST PUBLISHED JUNE 1983
REPRINTED SEPTEMBER 1983

Selected by the British Council for exhibition at the Frankfurt Book Fair in October 1983

Full colour reproductions of 19th century Irish watercolours on front and back cover.   Sewn binding.   115 pp.
ISBN 0 9503551 0 3   PRICE: £3.75

PORTMOON PRESS, PO Box 9, Limavady, BT49 9AJ, Northern Ireland

Frog Song

In February
From under the dangling leaves
Of tall eucalyptus trees
Along an Egyptian canal
Comes a chorus of quacks,
But no duck in sight;
Counter-tenor cats
Trill their falsetto purr;
Maniacs, hidden by the bank,
Laugh with staccato cackle;
Doors with rusty hinges
Incessantly creak .   .   .
The frogs are in voice again:
The season has begun.

Throaty diaphragms swell
On mud ledges;
Powerful hind legs
Become scissor-like projectiles
Into the safety
Of brown viscous water.

At the open-air restaurant
A blue-white light is an instrument of death
For mosquito and moth;
A popular restaurant with grill
For the population of the canal:
They line up with mouths open
While roasted delicacies drop in.

In August the song is over,
The frogs are silent.
It is left to cicadas
To fill the night air
With their music.

Cairo

Brown fingers and toes and striped dishdashas
Cling to the backs of bulging buses;
The crowds that throng Midan el Tahrir
Are a moving design: white shirts, black hair.
For miles along the river corniche
Traffic surges and fellaheen fish.
From the Nile an aquaduct climbs the hill
To the walls of Saladin's Citadel.
Within, an incongruous edifice:
Minarets and domes of a Turkish mosque.
Between here and the foot of Moqattam spread
The domed tombs of the City of the Dead.
Beyond Cairo in the Western Desert
Three pyramids sail into the sunset.

In *Pearl of the Sahara,* mosaic-patterned tent,
Belly-dancers gyrate to a mounting beat;
Trance-like skirted dervishes whirl,
Mesmerised bodies in space they swirl.
Moonlight gives way to *Son et Lumière*
On the staring Sphinx, enigmatic as ever.

In the city, an intimate café society,
Names come and go in sparkling variety;
Safeya, Nevine, Sheherezade,
Silvio, Sharif, Ali, Mohamed,
Rendezvous by night in Hotel Semiramis,
All day drink citron pressé in Groppi's,
See city lights from the Hilton Roof Bar,
Dance till they're dizzy in the Goha.
Milo, big spider in mediaeval web,
Keeps open house, Mameluke incarnate –
Galleried courtyards darkly connected,
Guarded by an old crone, half-demented,
Lead to a tall chamber, richly cushioned, dim,
A love-scene setting for an oriental film.

Kites mew above roof-top tenements,
Wheeling, looking for edible garbage.
Camels, donkeys, galabeyas, black veils,
Pass in and out of the old city walls.
Turbanned men enter through inscribed doorways
Cool, quiet mosques and kneel for their prayers.
In the Muski, copper-workers clang,
Pharaonic appliquéd cloth pictures hang.
Coin-bedecked embroidery of bedouin heirloom,
Silver rings, hinge-topped to hold perfume,
Amethyst, green, brown, hand-blown glass
With the bloom of a bubble, and coffee pots of brass,
Dimpled glass jars for pickled cucumber,
Tasselled gold necklaces, jade and amber:
Throughout the narrow alleyways milling
From east or west they are buying or selling.
Radios blare a sad Arab tune
The haunting voice of Umm Kalsum.

Flook

I forsook you, Flook,
You were my guard,
It was hard, pard;
I would not have you pine
In quarantine,
A desert dog
In London fog.

How well you leapt
Every time
To tug the washing
Off the line.
The shirts – oh boy –
With buttons – oh joy!
Around lemon and orange tree
Palm and poinsettia
My stockings trailed
And I wailed.
We strung them up higher
But you were
A high flyer.

Remember Crichton?
A Basset hound –
He cost his owners
Twenty pound.
"Ya Salaam!"
The gardener said
"I'd have got them a dog
With *proper* eyes and ears
Proper legs
And,
For *nothing!*"

You cost me nothing,
Flook.
You came from the pyramids
A beledi runt I took.
If it hadn't been
For your tail curled over
You might have been mistaken
For a golden labrador.
But golden you were
With long pedigree
A species rare
Of Pharaonic ancestry.

You woke me
From my siesta
You took me
Many a glad saunter.

How jealous you were
Of the gramophone
You wanted me
To be alone.

Sunday morning
In my arbour
Of carmine bougainvillea
You did not lie at my feet
You sat beside me on the seat
While I ate a sun-warm mango
Reflecting
It takes two to tango.

Remember Nabucco?
He was more fun
Than Crichton;
A big boxer fellow
There was good rough play
During his short stay.

How politely you smiled
At my friends;
Or at intruder snarled –
I could depend
On you.

How you tore up and down
By the trellis Morning Glory
As the camels padded by
And you barked furiously.
Where were you
On those nights away from home
And I was afraid you'd gone?
But that's another story.

With time, sorrow has been tempered
By an alleviating thought:
I would not mind
Being left behind
In Egypt.

Night Ride

Bridles jingle and clink –
Arab ponies arch their necks
To snatch at their bits
With snorts of excitement;
Hooves rustle in the sand
Hitting stray stones with a crack;
Saddles and stirrup leathers
Rhythmically creak:
Sounds unnoticed in the day
Dominate the night.

Hesperides

In Kyrenia harbour
The tip of a mast
Like a needle
Pierces a star.
A scimitar shines
On black marble water
Below the crescent moon.
Voices and laughter drift
Across the resinous night;
A watch glints on a bare wrist:
Two o'clock.
He throws back his head
To drink the last drop of Ouzo
Cock-er-i-ko! he cries
To the dark mountains.
A faint reply is heard
Cock-er-i-ko!
From village to village
In somnolent valleys
Sleepy cocks take up the cry
Cock-er-i-ko! Cock-er-i-ko!
He claps his friend on the shoulder –
Time to go.

Baghdad

The white Tigris reflects a dusty sky,
City noises echo across the water,
Car hooters play music concrète,
Muezzins sonorously howl to Allah.

Along the bund the pump is thumping –
Water for beanfields, water for clover;
Water buffalo wallow in a wadi
Or are they hippopotami?
Only their nostrils are visible
Exuding puffs of pleasure.
Black-veiled women, waterpots on heads,
Bare feet and bangles on ankles,
Disappear through courtyards into mud houses.
Doves gurgle from groves of palms
In the hot, humid air:
The date-ripening wind is here.

Follow the track and turn east
To the land of Sumer.
Mirages hover on the horizon:
Cities resurrected in a trick of light,
Civilisations lost under silt.
Like grit in a bucket of sand shaken
Relics have risen to the surface –
Votive offerings of clay: a chariot,
A ringlet-framed face, a paliasse.

Night is coming; turn west again
Across the pewter plate of desert
Under an apricot sky.
Follow the faint aroma of acrid dung fires
To the glow of the hidden furnace
Of the living city.

Isfahan

Blue cockscombs pierce the shining plateau,
Distant prospect from an ancient capital;
Beneath the many-arched galleried bridge
The river cascades over tiers of stone.

Tribes move north to summer pastures,
Long skirts swing below embroidered coats;
Hens cling to the camel's load,
New lambs are cradled in donkey panniers.

Shafts of sun through a low skylight
Light up a loom and a bright pile of skeins;
On a bench small girls with quick deft fingers
Fill up the bare warp, knot by knot.

A stranger wonderingly handles an astrolabe:
Brass discs engraved with centuries-old code;
Elsewhere in the spawning ground of chess
Shot taffeta vies with gaudy silk shawls.

In the shade of trees at the side of the Maidan
People drink leban from blue-green bowls –
Cool colour of sea for a hot arid land;
Turquoise tiles cover domes and walls.

Drumming hooves of the real polo players
Once kicked up dust where now we walk
By formal flowerbeds, lawns and pools,
And look up to the ghosts of the empty pavilion:

Timbered verandahs of Ali Qapu –
The sweet life speaks from painted rooms;
Openwork panelling will catch the music
Lest an echo should spoil its cadences.

A Persian Dream

Where are your proud king-builders now,
Persepolis?
Darius, Xerxes –
Do they revisit you sometimes
Like a desert wind
Drifting with sighs
Through the columns,
Skeleton doorways,
Fallen capitals,
Of your unroofed halls?

Do the emissaries
Of provincial satraps
Step from their carved relief
To wander the palace plateau
Descend its staircases
Return to their homelands
Saying
The Empire is no more?

The column of dust on the horizon
Was not a natural phenomenon
But an avalanche
Of men, horses, spears.
From his untimely death-tent
By the Euphrates
Did he ever regret, Alexander,
The sacking of Persepolis?

Tulips

Pointed petals, rounded base,
Vase-like blooms with narrow waist,
Ornament of Ottoman garden,
Perpetual artists' inspiration,
Twining tulips glazed in tiles
Growing on Islamic walls,
Woven into silk brocade,
Or jewelled embroidery made,
Richest rugs for Turkish palace –
Wonder of the Bosphorus –
Inlaid sword for noble Sultan,
Painted screens for his hareem:
By carriage from Constantinople
Came the precious bulb imperial.

The Return to London

Interminable escalator –
How many more bras and briefs
Do we have to endure?
The affluent society
Gives me a pain.
It gives itself a pain too:
Grey faces grooved with anxiety
Are hurrying, trying, buying,
Straining in the dripping rain.

Take me back to the sun
To smiling faces
Where the old are cared for,
Where the issue is not underwear
But one thing to wear;
Not what shall we eat
But shall we eat today;
Not which car, but bare feet.

London

City of subterranean movement –
Living masses surge through deep caverns,
Erupting from surface pot-holes
To spill unendingly over the streets.
Naturalistic lakes and a tracery of trees
Grace miniature landscapes artfully contrived:
Small sanctuaries encircled by the dust and grind
Of busy millions milling round and round.
Home of our language, poetically performed
In popular entertainment at the Globe;
Capital river, port and thoroughfare –
Ships have sailed from your leaden tides
To the bucking oceans of the outer world.

Tuning strings and a crowded murmur
Fill the tiered horse-shoe of the opera;
In scores of darkened auditoria
Silent faces watch as curtains rise.
Re-enactment of the antics of our species,
Spoken, sung or danced by painted people,
Fascinates the tribe inexhaustibly.

Feet and voices echo through museum emporium,
Depository of treasure trove and treasure taken:
Truth and beauty, loot and booty,
Magpie man has gathered trinkets for his nest.
Marble horses that once glistened above olive trees
Where bells of goats tinkled among spring flowers,
Are frozen in their frieze
Around a cold and alien chamber.

Towers of Babel, a multitude of tongues,
Differing customs dictate the costumes:
Cosmopolitan diversity, metropolitan zoo.
Spare a thought for our captive cousins,
Lustrous pelts, spotted, striped or mottled,
Animated architecture, squawking confectionery,
Prehensile tails, purpose-built snouts,
Giant strength, agility, perfect physique,
In their element stream-lined speed,
Intuitive intelligence, natural order –
It is not they but the puny human
Who should be caged until eventual extinction.

A Game of Squash

In a cubic drawing board
Two draughtsmen compete:
Surrealist pencils swirl
Above stampeding rubber feet.

The whack of the black speck
Echoes .   .   .
Silence as a drop shot
Makes a cobweb in a corner.

Hearts are pounding,
Stars before the eyes,
Wet-faced and scarlet
They exult in exercise.

Christmas Cards

Come to the party, wave the wand,
An Old Master apiece, a list in my hand –
The only occasion a harassed hostess
Without distraction may talk to each guest.
Plenty of space to scribble inside
The news of the year and more beside,
Enquire after family, gossip a bit;
They seem to be here, beside me they sit.
Chile, Brazil, New Zealand, Dubai,
Travel the world in my mind's eye.
A successful party, for day after day
Friends reappear and seem to stay:
They fill the room, we keep on meeting –
Oh happy, happy Christmas greeting.

Train of Thought

The waiting room can only wait
Beyond the little garden gate:
There are no trains to be late
    At this station.

No one comes here now to travel,
Grass is growing in the gravel,
The sprouting platform scarcely level
    For perambulation.

The trellis rose is overgrown,
Pebble-edged patches are not mown,
Pansies and marigolds are self-sown
    In natural fashion.

In full view just a field away
Trucks roar on the motorway;
Door to door is the way today
    Of transportation.

Ever wider, faster road,
Ever louder, vaster load –
Combustion chaos may bode
    Regeneration.

Full Moon

Moon, take me with you
Let me make
Ink shadows on paper fields
White light on the dark river
Luminous houses
Silhouettes of hills and trees
Pearly edges of unseen clouds
In a fathomless blue-black sky.

Moon, take me with you
Let me shine
On a coasting seagull and eerie cliffs
On a curve of sand and a cove of rocks
On seals asleep on a reef;
On foaming crests of the swell at sea
On a shoal of fish as they slither on deck
On the pale faces and hands of men.

Moon, take me with you
To another land
Where the desert air is warm, and sweet
With the scent of bean-flowers and village fires
And dust. Your light has dimmed the stars
In a perfect hemisphere of night;
Ancient temples gleam with ghostly beauty
And the yellow dogs are silent.

Moon, take me with you
Let me spin
In incomprehensible space,
Let me walk weightless
On your powdery ground,
With slow moon-strides explore the unexplored
Until blackness hides all.
Gravity, help me home.

Moon, take me with you
Let me sleep
In a moonlit bedroom, and dream
Of curious encounters,
Precarious heights,
Labyrinthine ruins, dissolving
Into downland; plummet like a lark,
Swim away in the pull of your tide.

The Horncarver

The daily turning of lathe and polisher
Upon cowhorn and staghorn of many seasons
Had transmuted his workshop
Into an eerie den, a cave of moon-dust,
With here and there a shining artefact
In muted shades of buff and onyx:
Horn beakers, of pre-war picnic renown,
Cornucopia, paper-knife, knee-high shoehorn.

From somewhere, as though by magic,
He lifted a violin, newly made, unvarnished,
So pale one doubted that it could
Emit the finished sound.
Raising it to his shoulder, the horncarver
Placed his dusty fingers on the strings.
Music came forth like a mountain stream –
Amber-clear in pools and eddies,
Leaves dropped into it and were borne away,
Dragonflies hovered over it,
Deer paused to drink at it,
Other streams joined it,
Until, far away, fanned out across the sand,
It lost itself in the sea.

He lowered the bow with a half-smile,
The inward smile of one who played for himself.
"What is the name of the tune?" I asked,
Hardly imagining that the mellifluous air
Possessed anything so mundane as a name.
"*Leaving Lismore*" he said.
I heard the sound of oars dipping,
The crunch and lap of waves on a hull.
I did not know, nor did he say,
Who left Lismore, nor why.

UNDER THE SKIN

Morning

Consciousness rose in a spiral,
A dark weed of trailing tendrils,
Uprooted from the deep sea bed
To slither and float
On a surface rippled
With the day's wind and tide.
Among the jetsam of numb limbs,
Upon a white wave face,
Dropped the feather flotsam
Of a soft kiss.

Cameo

In a lagoon
We idled
In blazing light
Time idled with us
The sand seared
Our bare feet
We found shade
Under a rock.
You said "I cannot imagine
Ever loving anyone else."
My heart was breaking
For another.
Breakers broke on coral
What a waste of you
What a waste of me
What a waste
Waste.

Mirage

The mosque seemed alone,
Without a minaret,
The sunrise tipped its domes –
A seductive silhouette.
Its walls were unviolated
By the foreign infidel;
It was pure and sacrosanct,
An unknown citadel.

A minaret appeared
In the haze above;
The muezzin mounted
For his call of love.
Columns and carpets
Faded away –
Mosque and minaret shimmered
In the white-hot day.

Checkmate

Handsome he was, bronze skin shining,
Lithe-muscled, exuberantly male,
Drawn as a night moth, window-pining,
To her, fair-haired and pale.

She was malleable, floury, a piece of dough,
Ripe to be rolled out, shaped by the chef,
A dish of passion fruit, nectarine, mango,
A free translation of her Saxon self –

An ivory queen, and she was taken
Early in the game. Inspired, devout,
Smooth as bishops – to serve the king
They tilted together as one knight.

Then there was play and counter-play of pawn;
On rook and castle broke a chequered dawn.

Uphill Love

What is life without variety and risk?
In love too we spurn the simple course,
Seeking returned affection where none is –
Dejection and black misery: prime source.

Love seems to like an uphill path,
Progressively ascending, by the challenge lured,
Recharging itself in the storm's aftermath,
Rewarded by the certainty of something shared.

Love on the level is too easy-going,
Though no less nostalgic, one's salad days,
And downhill love nowhere flowing:
How painful is too-easily-won praise.

Idle speculation stop! End this song –
Numberless exceptions will prove me wrong.

Blind Alley

Their eventual union
Seemed a foregone conclusion:
Mature, unattached,
A couple well-matched.

She loved his presence
Not perceiving its essence;
He liked his companion
But did not know women.
For her, two was company;
He preferred crowded safety.

She thought he was serious
But elusive, mysterious;
She dreamed of involvement –
He withheld the next instalment.
The clinch of dance
Threw him off balance.

Confusedly available
To a creature unattainable,
She took his hand –
It was like dead wood.
On parted ground
At last she understood.

A Woman thinks of her Lover

Dear heart – this beautiful spring day
Holds me in its embrace.
It smiles at me, invites me to take part,
And clouds lie soft on the hills.

Dear heart – if this same day
Surrounds you – take it and enjoy each moment of light.
Then we will be together, sharing this sun,
Linked by this ground between us.

Sweet Chestnut

My husk
My prickly outer cover
My dawn, my dusk
My humming summer's day
My lowering sky
My storms
My drifts of fallen leaves
My ground, my roots
My rampart against the world
My sleeping Winter
My sap, my Spring
My husband.

Husband and Wife

Horizontal conclusion
To a vertical week:
They recount their news,
With similar views
On the endemic daftness
Of their acquaintance.
Uncensored thoughts are voiced
In the comfortable dark,
Until some stirring topic –
Scientific, nostalgic,
Or worse, domestic –
Awakes one
And sends to sleep the other.

Do It Yourself

Old mortar falls from all around
Thick-walled windows;
Mildewed wallpaper comes off clean.
Sinister crevices, ceiling to floor,
Corner to corner,
Are revealed, and crawling creatures emerge.

An electric sander sears the silent day –
Dense whiteness fills the shrouded room:
Shades of a far-off forgotten dust storm,
One's teeth grate in fine silt.

An electric hammer-drill dynamites the brain –
Thoughts explode and fly in all directions;
An electric saw screams through timber –
Horror films flash behind the eyes.

Once upon a time, we are told,
Quiet men came with a leather hold-all;
These men have gone.
Their sons are side by side
In deep-litter assembly lines
Taking home their hundred basic.

A porcelain figurine on a dusty shelf:
Her glaze is crazed by Do It Yourself.

Requiem for a Tree

Trees are born free;
Everywhere men have chain saws.
I see
Power by proxy,
Clearance by the unseeing.
I hear
A tortured roar –
A king beast fights
For its life.
Generations pass
In as many silent seconds
Before the crescendo
Of the crash.
I grieve
For death without cause.

Water Buffalo

My father used to say
That water buffalo,
Dragging a bent branch
To plough the dust,
Had two speeds:
Dead slow and stop.
Could it be
At the tender age
Of two or three
Their character
Entered me?

Inertia

Reluctant waker, open both eyes,
Bring the day into focus,
Cast off the feathers that weigh you down
And stand up, lest the dream go on.

Life goes by on the other side of the glass,
Here dust is inert, an atmosphere of moon,
A beetle on its back
Unable to turn over and move on.

Grass grows under the feet,
Moss gathers on this motionless stone,
Procrastination has stolen the time,
Put off until tomorrow, because today
        doesn't seem to be here.

Depth of Field

Was the sun so bright that afternoon
Were the hills really so clear
Shall I ever forget the navy-blue sea
And the grassy-fragrant air?

Lenticular clouds in a fairy-tale sky,
How sharply engraved each tree:
Clarity, oh for the clarity –
When you loved me.

Eyes are veiled like a misty day,
Mind – a hidden mountain;
Feet as heavy as fallen scree –
Gone, exhilaration.

Off Day

Today seems new –
I haven't seen it before.
Someone says hallo
As though they knew me;
There must have been other days –
Wonder where they went to?

Before this one disappears,
Let's have a look at it:
The detail is good,
Very sharp in fact; but
The perspective seems strange,
And the people larger than life.
Don't think I'll buy it –
Show me something else.

In Two Minds

One half makes the decision,
The other half wonders why;
Gregarious and Flamboyant
Held back by Solitary and Shy.

A house gives way to silence,
By a dreaming mind overtaken;
Daydreams are sown in welcoming earth
When dormant green fingers rewaken.

The sensuous soul is cat-like,
A creature of silky sloth;
The practical side with a puritan streak
Thrives on the work of both.

The aesthete receives impressions
In tones of light and sound;
The do-er's driving force grapples
With raw stuff on the ground.

The scholar absorbs with interest
All manner of information;
The voluptuary seeks in other ways
More entertaining relaxation.

The sower of wild oats luxuriates
In unheeding eccentricity;
The committed spouse is diligent
In irreproachable domesticity.

One likes physical exercise
In organised intricate sport;
The other alone in the natural world
Finds strength of a different sort.

Right is calm and caring,
Responsible, kind and zealous;
Left: unpredictable as the ocean –
Turbulent, caustic and callous.

"I am me"

Her puzzled personality said "I am me",
Defining but one aspect of the case;
Only the deluded think that they are free –
Accept it or no, we occupy a place.

We are our parents' child, from youth to age,
Reversing rôles in mid-term as their powers wane;
A sibling's fellow in the family cage,
A spouse's spouse: a parent of our children.

Towards others we are of variable mien –
Talk, listen, lean, support, avoid, confide.
Past and present make a compound being;
A smiling face may untold anguish hide.

Upon our core these diverse strains impinge,
Less thought about the better, lest the mind unhinge.

She Sighs

She sighs for what does not exist,
For happiness that never was;
Not having lost, yet feels a loss,
Despite herself, an optimist.

Her mirror image cries "Desist!
From hungering desire, have pause;
Let cool content replace will-force,
Be philosophic, pessimist."

Life's lathe has left her roughly finished,
Turned, as it were, against the grain;
A talent despoiled, or one diminished.

What polished piece she might have been;
But character is not extinguished –
Like earth rotates, and is the same again.

Seamstress

I cannot choose
My cloth of time
It may be heavy or light
Soft or rough
Patterned or plain
It may be wrong or right.

How shall I cut
My cloth of time
Will it be long or short?
How shall I sew it –
Bit by bit
Or one seam throughout?

How will it fit
My made-up cloth –
Revealing or disguise?
A strait-jacket
A carefree shift
A hell or paradise?

How shall I wear
My robe of time
Routinely or with flair?
What kind of image
Will it give –
Strait-laced or devil-may-care?

How shall I play
Life's pantomine –
Will I sing or dance or fly?
Will anyone notice
That I am there,
As the scene goes by?

Where is the end
Of the cloth of time
Will it unroll for ever?
Can I not choose
The warp and woof
Can I not be the weaver?

Sandcastle

He was a welcome guest at my sandcastle,
As I patted it into shape,
Even suggesting small embellishments
That I could make.

She was not an accommodating visitor,
Nor I a happy host;
A spadeful here, a spadeful there -
My castle lost.

I was glad to watch it dissolve
As the tide whispered over the sand:
"It's risky, risky to allow a looker-on
The upper hand."

Spring Blues

Yellow flowers flaunt,
Emerald leaves haunt,
Plump buds push,
Song birds gush.

Season of reminder –
Nothing unkinder;
Forget regret,
Live life yet.

Nothing as young
As new grass sprung,
Nor as ideal
As a petal;

Nothing as worthy
As a tree,
Growing strong
To live long.

A Weed's Lament

I may be a weed but I don't need
Caustic weedkiller on my head:
Every seed has a right to breed,
Why should I be dead?

I grow willy-nilly, no rarefied lily,
Nor ravishing, radiant poppy;
My petals aren't frilly, I'm a hill-billy,
With a tendency to be stroppy.

I take my chance in poor circumstance,
But prefer rich earth of opportunity
Where I may enhance my natural advance,
If not nipped by frosty animosity.

I may be a devil but I will shrivel
In a long drought of indifference,
Or in stony soil of disapproval,
If not drowned in a flood of interference.

Like any plant what I really want
Is a climate of affection,
With rain sent for encouragement,
And the sunshine of admiration.

Women's Fib

Alas, she has no profession,
No way of making life pay;
Doomed to domestic oppression
Until the end of the day.

Alas, she has no objection,
No liberation revolt;
A comfortably kept woman
Unlikely ever to bolt.

In her there is no ambition,
No nagging desire to be free;
She likes the idea of freedom
But not responsibility.

She has no determination,
No passion to make her name;
In her limited imagination
All jobs seem much the same.

In her there is no confusion,
No crisis of unattained power;
Undeterred by propagandist derision
She watches her garden flower.

Animus

Anger in the air, by Jove,
Anger in air;
Brows are knitted, teeth are gritted:
Anger in the air.

Civilised discussion ends
As the poison pall descends –
Faces whiten, faces redden,
Muscles tighten, feelings deaden;
Anger in the air.

In the acrid atmosphere
Breath is short, the eyes dilate;
Indifference, discord and hate –
Anger in the air.

Souls despair in hostile aura,
Shy ones shrink, the fearless fight;
Minds recoil, their springs wound tight:
Anger in the air.

Animals will turn away
When anger fills the air;
Monster unfed is monster dead,
And clear again the air.

Thoughts from a Chinese Province

I

It is good to be busy; it is good also to have leisure –
They follow each other as winter follows summer.
In between are autumn and spring,
The seasons of preparation and transition.
This morning I thought that rain was falling, in heavy drops,
But it was leaves, fluttering like gold birds from my tulip tree,
Released by a touch of frost last night.
They form a lustrous carpet on the ground,
A priceless gift which I receive with joy every year.
For many months I have worked in the garden;
Now it is time to light the fire and sit with my books,
Making journeys in my mind to far-off countries.
I hear my gate opening – I hope it is a friend,
For then we can enjoy a glass of wine together
And share our random reflections.

II

A painting will capture the imagination
If its colour and line are subtly combined
And form a composition inexplicably right.
Then it will draw one in, to come closer,
To examine and admire the invisible skill.

A poster will catch the attention of passers-by;
Having done so, it has something to say,
And says it boldly and with style.
It uses but few words, in a striking phrase,
To ensure that people will remember the message.
The passer-by does not examine the poster –
He walks on, thinking about other matters,
Noticing perhaps a girl's face, petal-like,
Or the tawny sunset reflected in puddles in the street.

As with the artist, so with the poet;
His poem may resemble a painting
Because he has caught a feeling, and put it on paper.
Or he may be like a graphic artist –
One can read his words and understand the meaning
But the spirit has darted away.

In Praise of Imperfection

Imperfection pleases every time –
Irregular rhythm, inexact rhyme;
The steady drum will dull and deaden,
Rather dance to irresistible syncopation.
Music swells with imperceptible pause,
Great art follows indefinable laws.
In a garden where weeds grow,
Rare and unexpected seedlings show;
Find among unscheduled leisure
Nuggets of hitherto unknown pleasure.
Detachedly marvel at flawless beauty
But enjoy the charm of originality;
Admire in a person of wayward spirit
Imagination and inventive wit.
Too precise a pattern in house or dress
Seems an avoidance of natural choice.
Let life an equivalent course follow –
No trailing ant, but erratic swallow.

FAIR GAME

A Soggy Sense of Ireland

Lines inspired by a distinguished contemporary

Birth of a Zoologist

I delve
in the river.
A glut
of slimy elver

fills my uninitiated hand.
Fingers are eels
flicking. It peels
its pullulating skin, shucks

its sleek shape –
plick plock pluck
into the slick muck
by the blocked lock

the naked silver
slithers.

Mudlark

Thick boots squelch while
ploughed furrows envelop
with sludgy dollop.
Will o' the wisp belches

from the belly of the bog
as the keen blade
of a spade pierces
eternity.

I hear the heave, groan,
slap, suck, moan
of the earth's
fecundity;

mud
in its measureless
profundity
embraces me.

Wallowing About

Cowpats splatter on concrete yard;
An eruption of steam spurts
From each wet sculpted nostril
Of primaeval quadrupeds

Breathing hard.
Time to milk.
Pneumatic pink udder
With pale hairs of silk

Induces a townsman's shudder.
Warm sickly smell squirts
Into enamel bucket.
He claps a skeletal hand

On a lanky Friesian flank:
Move over,
Cloven-hooved sustainer
Of a cloven people.

Encompass Me

Collude with me,
   be wooed by me,
Seclude me,
   canoodle me,
Best of all
   occlude me –
Impolder
   me.

Peeled Word

The salty name
lingers:
Portstewart –

Port: bollarded harbour
where my tongue
seeks the deep
fulfilment of

– stew: our native
delicacy
greasy
but true

– art, no less,
that binds us
together
in our bewilderness.

Scoffchops

Scoffchops is the scourge of the neighbourhood,
Others hide as he stalks by;
Those who dare to meet him, face to face,
More fool they.

Scoffchops looks like a wild cat –
Striped, with leopard-spotted front:
Perfectly camouflaged for whatever
Nefarious hunt.

Scoffchops washes his gory whiskers,
He scratches his battered ears,
He licks his rabbit-flavoured paws, and thinks –
The little dears.

Scoffchops is only a gentleman
In so far as he is not a lady;
Merely lying in the sun he looks
Very shady.

Scoffchops has a silky female friend,
Her favours are much in demand;
He disposed of superfluous suitors
And won her hand.

Scoffchops enjoys a father's duties –
Babysitting, discipline, hunting drill;
In virtuoso demonstrations of every art
He shows his skill.

Scoffchops occupies the best armchair,
He gets food at a twitch of his tail;
Nobody knows quite how he does it –
Is it blackmail?

Wuffer

Wuffer was liver-and-white.
Was he a spaniel? No, not quite;
His legs were short and his ears stood up
Except the tip, a velvety flap.
His tail was long, his lower jaw brief,
Pale amber eyes, a natural thief.

Eat an apple, and he drooled
Waiting for the juicy core:
He chewed it up and neatly left
Brown pips and stalk upon the floor.

Foreign Service

"An ambassador is an honest man sent
to lie abroad for the good of his country."

Sir Henry Wotton, 1604

The Consul's daughter is a good-time girl,
She has two Third Secretaries to keep her on the whirl;
Will she withhold her favours from Harry – or from Ray?
Informed Embassy opinion says "That'll be the day."

The Head of Chancery is looking rather listless,
His wife's away on leave, so he is socially defenceless;
There are parties on the rooftops, parties on the river,
Bush telegraph says he is home for breakfast hardly ever.

The talent in the typing pool is scarcely up to scratch:
In months of fraught liaisons they have not achieved a match;
Though Jenny might have got there, with her Russian Naval Captain,
But was on the next plane home – an affair of short duration.

The Press Officer's girlfriends seem to be a trifle shady;
They called him in and said to him "About this Polish lady,
Is it true, as we have heard, that you have slept with her?"
His reply, which saved his bacon, was "Frankly, I can't remember."

First Secretary and lovely wife are frightfully on the make,
At diplomatic parties they are known as "Double Take";
Their conversation, as they perform their separate circulation,
Is a smiling, systematic, cross-examination.

The Military Attaché has an unassuming demeanour,
His official calls in Scottish kilt invariably bewilder;
The band plays at the garden party, mosquitoes whine in trees,
His loving wife is seen to rub repellent on his knees.

The Air Attaché hankers for the life of active service,
Surreptitious beers are brought each morning to his office;
He was given a friendly flight in a local flying club Auster,
But his motives were mistrusted: he was buzzed down by a fighter.

The Visa Officer can warn of impending revolution
From the sharp increase in customers for U.K. medical attention;
Last time the mob arrived, tear gas was at the ready,
No secret documents remained: they were carbon up the chimney.

Administration Officer is trying to curb the racket:
The private sale of motor cars is making quite a packet;
New regulations have arrived, bound with Treasury red tape,
But the wise A.O. will stall until he's made his own escape.

Second Secretary Commercial is an ex-colonial golden bowler,
Now he's painting local scenes in charming water colour;
British businessmen who visited his latest exhibition
Have reported excellent sales and very little competition.

The aristocratic Counsellor adores the ancien régime,
He was previously in Paris where he knew the crème de la crème;
At his soirées half the guests are missing, the remainder rather pale:
Their property's been sequestrated or they've been put in jail.

The Ambassador's reporting is not as good as Reuters;
(His novelist wife likes the setting for her stories)
A man of pride, he'd like to bear a heavier White Man's Burden,
But when something seems important, they send out a chap from London.

The Snore

The triffle, the squiffle,
The trumpet involuntary,
The tentative tremor,
The full-fledged roar;
The gargle, the bubble,
The rise and fall commentary,
The garbled murmur,
The all-night snore.

The waffle, the sniffle,
The night documentary,
The grunt, the whimper,
The unfeline purr;
The gasp, the chuckle,
The snort supplementary,
The audible dreamer,
The eight-hour bore.

Working Woman

Goodbye leisure
Goodbye the ad hoc life
Got to earn a living
Goodbye to being a wife.

Goodbye marmalade
Goodbye the home-made wine
Got to stir up paper
Goodbye sunshine.

Goodbye, whiskered friends
Goodbye, chestnut tree
Got to perch in an office
Goodbye to being free.

Goodbye, happy hermit
Goodbye the lazy browse
Got to work, hermetically sealed,
Goodbye, grass and cows.

Goodbye, the morning garden
Goodbye earth and seed
Got to clock in, clock in,
Goodbye the small-hours read.

Goodbye, rainy day
Goodbye the put-off chore
Got a good excuse now
Goodbye, open door.

Goodbye, lord and master
Goodbye, the wifely rôle
Got to share the honours now
Goodbye, female soul.

Poet's Creed

I'm a poet
I know it
I don't conceal
How I feel
Nor shun
Attention –
My game
Is to declaim,
My arsenal
Personal,
My inspiration
Titillation.
My clientèle
Can't tell
Hocus
From pocus;
My technique
May be weak,
No word
Too absurd –
I lure
By being obscure.
I'm like strobe
As I probe –
Every caper
Goes on paper,
Every thought
Can be bought,
My muse
Is news,
Free verse
A gold purse,
The mundane
My gain.
I transform
The norm,
I uncover
The lover,
I harbour
The macabre,
I have hoarded
The sordid.
I'm a poet
So I owe it
To posterit
y to do it.

EPILOGUE

Memsahib

Pebbles from an Indian sandpit

When I was young, my mother was young too,
Tall and slim, with wavy auburn hair cut in a fashionable bob,
And elegantly dressed.
As a bride she came to India;
In her luggage were six evening dresses,
Ten white nightdresses, of linen lawn, and silk,
Any number of dainty pointed shoes,
Some of them in colours matching the dresses,
And a fancy dress costume for wearing on board ship:
A Dresden shepherdess, turquoise silk with panniers
Over latticed pink satin, gold lace elbow frills,
A powdered wig with ringlets, and silver crook with yellow bow.
She has it all still, packed in tissue paper in a cabin trunk.
Spotted silk afternoon dresses she wore, with floppy brimmed hats,
And a beautifully tailored brown riding habit with boots
When on her mare Belinda, in the cool of the day
At four in the morning.
The boots had tight-fitting wooden trees
And stood in our attic in England for years
Looking strangely disembodied,
Though less so than the sad leopard skin
Mounted on dark blue felt, complete with paws, claws and snarling head.
He was not shot by anyone, but was accidentally run over by a train
As he lay asleep on the railway track.

For fifteen years my father built railways in India
And bridges across wadis and rivers.
Many men were required for the work because there were no big machines
Each man carried just a small amount of earth in the basket on his head –
It was too hot and he was too thin to do any more.
In the cool season they were too cold to work at all;
They huddled in corners wrapped in anything they could find
And waited for warm days to come again.
Frequently my parents lived in a railway saloon, mahogany-panelled,
Or in a tent;

Wherever it was, there were servants to prepare meals,
Albeit sometimes of an indeterminate goaty-muttony-beefy-steak variety.
My staple diet was bananas
And buffalo milk cunningly disguised with cocoa
To entice me to drink it.
Some years later it was explained to me
That engineer did not mean engine driver.

Adults and children alike wore topees in the sun.
My father's Bearer was a kind and handsome Sikh,
Tremendously smart in his high-necked white suit and turban.
My Ayah was plump and swathed in white muslin;
She sat all day and I climbed all over her.
I had a sandpit under trees behind the grass tennis court,
A doll's house on the verandah,
And a tiled square sunken bath in one of the shady rooms
Of our spacious high-ceilinged bungalow.
Fine wire mesh over the plughole kept out snakes.
An enormous monkey ambled in one day
Heading for a pile of fruit arranged for a dinner party.
My mother threw a loaf of bread at him – he caught it
And made off into the bushes, looking pleased.

When I was in bed, my mother came to kiss me goodnight
Before she went to a dinner party.
She smelt nice, and let me stroke her evening fur
And I went to sleep happy.
My mother thought that Indian ladies were the most elegant of all,
With their butterfly-coloured saris,
Sleek hair and graceful walk.
One of them had a daughter aged two or three, like me,
Who sometimes came to play.
My brother was five or six, and had certain perks:
One of these was an elephant to ride on,
Which caused me undying envy.
A Maharajah friend had a pack of foxhounds;
Most splendid he looked, sitting white-turbanned on his white horse
At the start of the meet.

My father was nicknamed Kruschen, after the salts,
Because of his energy. If he was not working,
He was playing polo, squash, tennis, golf, pig-sticking or shooting,
All of which were supposed to prevent people from getting "liverish".
In knee-length shorts and knee-socks, fawn or white,
He looked rather dashing.
I sat on his knee while he read to me from one of my two books
Which I knew by heart: Peter Rabbit and Little Black Sambo.
Nobody in those days thought the latter was tactless or racist;
I always felt sorry for the tigers who turned into ghee.

Occasionally from up-country we visited Bombay.
The flat had marble floors;
There was a gramophone with a trumpet
As in the picture for His Master's Voice.
A record played the Gold and Silver Waltz,
A favourite tune at the Bombay Yacht Club
Where my parents danced under the stars.

Work was not altogether unheard-of for my mother.
Certain domestic jobs were above one caste but below another,
So she did them herself.
Sometimes in remote places the days seemed long;
For something to do she unpicked the seams of a dress
And used it as a pattern to make a new one
With cloth from the bazaar.

A child in our syce's family died of smallpox.
A colleague died of rabies, another of malaria.
My brother lost all his hair through ringworm;
Miraculously it grew again.
Aged five, he went on a solo trip in a rickety Bombay lift
And got stuck between floors.
He was rescued unhurt by an Indian lad who was skinny enough
To climb up and squeeze into the iron lift cage.

In the hot season wives and children left the plains for the hills,
A day's journey by train, zig-zagging up and up
Until poor Ayah was sick.
All I can remember about the Himalayas is that a large ball
That I was playing with rolled down a mountain, out of sight.
I couldn't go and get it because, my father said,
There were bears down there.
It was some consolation to think that the bears had my ball.

Home leave was every three years.
In alternate years wives went home with children
Leaving husbands behind.
Or they went home to have babies, as my mother did,
Returning proudly with the new member of the family
When it was a few months old.
All sorts of strange parties took place on the ship
To fill in the three-week voyage.
Father Neptune was hauled on board, covered with seaweed –
I hid behind my mother; other children cried and screamed.
There was a swimming pool on deck, into which tiny tots including me
Jumped happily and did spontaneous dog-paddle around watchful mothers.
On return from leave our Ayahs and Bearers were waiting for the ship
At the Bombay dockside, with garlands of flowers and a big welcome.

As school age arrived, it was goodbye to India
For some reason that I have never discovered,
Except that it was the custom of the time.
What better education could any child have had
Than to grow up in that serene but seething continent?
Possibly it was something to do with the fact
That my brother spoke Hindustani in preference to English
And was fluently profane.
So back it was, not to our own Ireland but to England,
To a small town near London and green downs and wartime.
My once-leisurely mother armed with ration books and bicycle
Divided her time between shop queues and kitchen chores.
We slept in a garden dug-out and ran to and fro in tin hats.

Now she is eighty, a widow, her children married and living elsewhere.
All that remains of her India are several albums of photographs
Neatly captioned in white ink on thick black paper;
A pair of sunset-and-palm-tree watercolours, painted by a friend,
Brass begging bowls and slender curving coffee pot,
And a collection of mixed but mostly happy memories.

For the small girl grown up,
India is a smell of dust, and spice,
A dun-coloured land of brilliant smiles,
A family compound
Where unhurried people come and go.